33 Ways of developing Khushoo' in Salaah

{ENGLISH}

33 سببا للخشوع في الصلاة

(الإنجليزية)

By:

Sheikh Muhammed Salih Al-Munajjid

Contents   Page

1. Introduction   3
2. Concealment of Khushoo'   4
3. Rulings on Khushoo'   6
4. The means of developing Khushoo'   8
5. Knowing the advantages of Khushoo' in Salaah   27
6. Warding off distractions and things that adversely affect khushoo   31
7. When a person suffers a great deal of waswaas   39
8. Conclusion   41

In the Name of Allah, Most Gracious Most Merciful

Introduction

Praise be to Allah, Lord of the Worlds, Who has said in His book (interpretation of the meaning), "...and stand before Allah with obedience" [al-Baqarah 2:238] and has said concerning the prayer (interpretation of the meaning): "... and truly it is extremely heavy and hard except for al-khaashi'oon..." [Al-Baqarah 2:45]; and peace and blessings be upon the leader of the pious, the chief of al-khaashi'oon, Muhammad the Messenger of Allah, and on all his family and companions.

Salaah is the greatest of the practical pillars of Islam, and khushoo' in prayer is required by sharee'ah. When Iblees, the enemy of Allah, vowed to mislead and tempt the sons of Adam and said "Then I will come to them from before them and behind them, from their right and from their left..." [al-A'raaf 7:17, interpretation of the meaning], one of his most significant plots became to divert people from salaah by all possible means and to whisper to them during their prayer so as to deprive them of the joy of this worship and cause them to lose the reward for it. As khushoo' will be the first thing to disappear from the earth, and we are living in the last times, the words of Hudhayfah (may Allah be pleased with him) are particularly pertinent to us: "The first thing of your religion that you will lose is khushoo', and the last thing that you will lose of your religion is salaah. There may be a person praying who has no goodness in him, and soon you will enter the mosque and not find anyone who has khushoo'." (al-Madaarij, 1/521).

Because of what every person knows about himself, and because of the complaints that one hears from many people about waswaas (insinuating thoughts from Shaytan) during the salaah and the loss of khushoo', the need for some discussion of this matter is quite obvious. The following is a reminder to myself and to my Muslim brothers, and I ask Allah to make it of benefit.

Allah says (interpretation of the meaning): "Successful indeed are the believers, those who offer their salaah (prayers) with all solemnity and full submissiveness." [al-Mu'minoon 23:1-2] - i.e., fearing Allah and in a calm manner. Khushoo' means calmness, serenity, tranquility, dignity and humility. What makes a person have this khushoo' is fear of Allah and the sense that He is always watching. (Tafseer Ibn Katheer, Daar al-Sha'b edn., 6/414). Khushoo' means that the heart stands before the Lord in humility and submission. (al-Madaarij, 1/520).

It was reported that Mujaahid said: "'...and stand before Allah with obedience" [al-Baqarah 2:238 - interpretation of the meaning]' - part of obedience is to bow, to be solemn and submissive, to lower one's gaze and to humble oneself out of fear of Allah, may He be glorified." (Ta'zeem Qadr al-Salaah, 1/188).

The site of khushoo' is the heart, and its effects are manifested in the physical body. The various faculties follow the heart: if the heart is corrupted by negligence or insinuating whispers from Shaytan, the worship of the body's faculties will also be corrupt. The heart is like a king and the faculties are like his troops who follow his orders and go where they are commanded. If the king is deposed, his followers are lost, which is like what happens when the heart does not worship properly.

Making a show of khushoo' is condemned. Among the signs of sincerity are:

Concealment of khushoo'

Hudhayfah (may Allah be pleased with him) used to say: "Beware of the khushoo' of hypocrisy." He was asked, "What is the khushoo' of hypocrisy?" He said, "When the body shows khushoo' but there is no khushoo' in the heart." **Fudayl ibn 'Ayaad said:** "It was disliked for a man to show more khushoo' than he had in his heart." **One of them saw a man showing khushoo' in his shoulders and body, and said,** "O So and so, khushoo' is here" – and he pointed to his chest, "not here" – and he pointed to his shoulders. (al-Madaarij, 1/521)

Ibn al-Qayyim (may Allah have mercy on him) said, explaining the difference between the khushoo' of true faith and the khushoo' of hypocrisy: "The khushoo' of true faith is when the heart feels aware and humble before the greatness and glory of Allah, and is filled with awe, fear and shyness, so that the heart is utterly humbled before Allah and broken, as it were, with fear, shyness, love and the recognition of the blessings of Allah and its own sins. So no doubt the khushoo' of the heart is followed by the khushoo' of the body. As for the khushoo' of hypocrisy, it is something that is put on with a great show, but there is no khushoo' in the heart. One of the Sahaabah used to say, 'I seek refuge with Allah from the khushoo' of hypocrisy." It was said to him, 'What is the khushoo' of hypocrisy?' He said, "When the body appears to have khushoo' but there is no khushoo' in the heart.' The person who truly feels khushoo' before Allah is a person who no long feels the flames of physical desire; his heart is pure and is filled with the light of the greatness of Allah. His own selfish desires have died because of the fear and awe which have filled his heart to overflowing so that his physical faculties have calmed down, his heart has become dignified and feels secure in Allah the remembrance of Him, and tranquillity descends upon him from his Lord. So he has become humble (mukhbit) before Allah, and the one who is humble is the one who is assured. Land that is "mukhbit" is land that is low-lying, in which water settles, so the heart that is "mukhbit" is humble and content, like a low-lying spot of land into which water flows and settles. The sign of this is that a person prostrates to his Lord out of respect and humility, and never raises his head until he meets Him. The arrogant heart, on the other hand, is one that is content with its arrogance and raises itself up like an elevated portion of land in which water never settles. This is the khushoo' of true faith."

As for overdoing it, and the khushoo' of hypocrisy, this is the attitude of a person who tries to make a great show of khushoo', but deep down he is still filled with desires. So on the outside he appears to have khushoo', but the snake of the valley and the lion of the forest reside within him, watching for prey. (Al-Rooh, p. 314, Daar al-Firk edn., Jordan).

"Khushoo' in prayer happens when a person empties his heart for it (prayer), and focuses on it to the exclusion of all else, and prefers it to everything else. Only then does he find comfort and joy in it, as the Prophet (peace and blessings of Allah be upon him) said: '… and my joy has been made in salaah.'" (Tafseer Ibn Katheer, 5/456. The hadith is in Musnad Ahmad, 3/128 and Saheeh al-Jaami', 3124).

Allah has mentioned al-khaashi'eena wa'l-khaashi'aat (men and women who are humble (before their Lord)), and described this quality as one of the qualities of those who are chosen. He tells us that He has prepared for them forgiveness and a great reward (i.e., Paradise). [See al-Ahzaab 33:35].

One of the benefits of khushoo' is that it makes prayer easier for a person. Allah tells us (interpretation of the meaning): "And seek help in patience and al-salaah (the prayer), and truly it is extremely heavy and hard except for al-khaashi'oon [i.e., the true believers, those who obey Allah with full submission, fear much from His Punishment, and believe in His Promise and in His Warnings]" [al-Baqarah 2:45]. The meaning is that the burden of prayer is heavy indeed, except for those who have khushoo'. (Tafseer Ibn Katheer, 1/125). Khushoo' is very important, but it is something that is easily lost and is rarely seen, especially in our own times, which are the last times. The Prophet (peace and blessings of Allah be upon him) said: "The first thing to be lifted up (taken away) from this ummah will be khushoo', until you will see no one who has khushoo'." (Al-Haythami said in al-Majma', 2/136: It was reported by al-Tabaraani in al-Kabeer, and its isnaad is hasan. See also Saheeh al-Targheeb, no. 543. He said it is saheeh).

......

Rulings on Khushoo'

According to the most correct view, khushoo' is obligatory. Shaykh al-Islam [Ibn Taymiyah], may Allah have mercy on him, said: "Allah, may He be exalted, says (interpretation of the meaning): 'And seek help in patience and al-salaah (the prayer), and truly it is extremely heavy and hard except for al-khaashi'oon ...' [al-Baqarah 2:45]. This implies condemnation of those who are not khaashi'oon... Condemnation only applies when something obligatory is not done, or when something forbidden is done. If those who do not have khushoo' are to be condemned, this indicates that khushoo' is obligatory (waajib)... The fact that khushoo' is obligatory is also indicated by the aayaat (interpretation of the meaning): 'Successful indeed are the believers, those who offer their salaah (prayers) with all solemnity and full submissiveness... These are indeed the inheritors, who shall inherit the Firdaws (Paradise). They shall dwell therein forever.' [al-Mu'minoon 23:1-2, 10-11] Allah, may He be glorified and exalted, tells us that these are the ones who will inherit Firdaws (Paradise), which implies that no-one else will do so... Khushoo' is obligatory in prayer, and this includes calmness and khushoo' [the original says 'khushoo'; perhaps what is meant is khudoo' meaning submission, humility]. Whoever pecks like a crow in his sujood (prostration) does not have khushoo', and whoever does not raise his head fully from rukoo' (bowing) and pause for a while before going down into sujood is not calm, because calmness implies doing things at a measured pace, so the person who does not do things at a measured pace is not calm. Whoever is not calm does not have khushoo' in his rukoo' or sujood, and whoever does not have khushoo' is a sinner... Another indication that khushoo' in prayer is obligatory is the fact that the Prophet (peace and blessings of Allah be upon him) warned those who do not have khushoo', such as the one who lifts up his gaze to the sky (in prayer), because this movement and raising of the gaze goes against the idea of khushoo'..." (Majma' al-Fataawa, 22/553-558).

Concerning the virtues of khushoo' and as a warning to the one who neglects it, the Prophet (peace and blessings of Allah be upon him) said: "Five prayers which Allah has made obligatory. Whoever does wudoo' properly for them, prays them on time, does rukoo' properly and has perfect khushoo', it is a promise from Allah that he will be forgiven, but whoever does not do this, has no such promise – if Allah wishes, He will forgive him, and if He wishes, He will punish him." **(Reported by Abu Dawood, no. 425; Saheeh al-Jaami', 3242).**

Concerning the virtues of khushoo', the Prophet (peace and blessings of Allah be upon him) also said: "Whoever does wudoo' and does it well, then prays two rak'ahs focusing on them completely [according to another report: and does not think of anything else], will be forgiven all his previous sins [according to another report: will be guaranteed Paradise]." (Al-Bukhari, al-Bagha edn., no. 158; al-Nisaa'i, 1/95; Saheeh al-Jaami', 6166).

When we look at the things that help us to have khushoo' in prayer, we find that they may be divided into two types: things that help you to have and to strengthen khushoo', and warding off the things that reduce and weaken khushoo'. Shaykh al-Islam Ibn Taymiyah (may Allah have mercy on him) explained the things that help us to have khushoo':

"Two things help us to [develop khushoo']: a strong desire to do what is obligatory, and weakness of distractions.

With regard to the first, the strong desire to do what is obligatory:

[this means that] a person strives hard to focus on what he is saying and doing, pondering on the meanings of the Qur'an recitation, dhikr and du'aa's, and keeping in mind the fact that he is speaking to Allah as if he sees Him, for when he is standing in prayer, he is talking to his Lord.

Ihsaan means 'that you worship Allah as if you see Him, and if you cannot see Him, He can see you.' The more the slave tastes the sweetness of salaah, the more attracted he will be to it, and this has to do with the strength of his imaan.

The means of strengthening imaan are many, and this is why the Prophet (peace and blessings of Allah be upon him) used to say, 'In your world, women and perfume have been made dear to me, and my joy is in prayer.' According to another hadith, he said, 'Let us find comfort in prayer, O Bilaal' – he did not say, 'Let us get it over and done with.'

With regard to the second, weakness of distractions:

This means striving to push away all distractions that make you think of something other than the prayer itself, and warding off thoughts that keep you mind off the purpose of the prayer. This is something which differs from one person to another, because the extent of waswaas has to do with the extent of one's doubts and desires and the heart's focus and dependence on what it loves, and its efforts to avoid what it dislikes." (Majmoo' al-Fataawa, 22/606-607)

On the basis of this division, we will now discuss some of:

The means of developing Khushoo'

1 – Striving to gain that which gives and strengthens khushoo'

This can be achieved in several ways, such as the following:

Preparing oneself for prayer properly

For example:

By repeating the words of the adhaan after the muezzin;

By pronouncing the du'a' to be recited after the adhaan: "Allaahummah Rabba haadhihi'l-da'wati'l-taammah wa'-salaati'l-qaa'imah, aati Muhammadan il-waseelata wa'l-fadeelah, wab'ath-hu'l-maqaam al-mahmood alladhi wa'adtah (O Allah, Lord of this perfect call and the prayer to be offered, grant Muhammad the privilege (of interceding) and also the eminence, and resurrect him to the praised position that You have promised)";

Reciting du'a' between the adhaan and the iqaamah;

Doing wudoo' properly, saying Bismillaah before it and making dhikr and saying the du'a' after it, "Ash-hadu an laa ilaaha ill-Allah wahdahu laa shareeka lah wa ash-hadu anna Muhammadan 'abduhu wa rasooluhu (I bear witness that there is no god except Allah alone, with no partner or associate, and I bear witness that Muhammad is His slave and messenger)" and "Allaahummaj'alni min al-tawwaabeena waj'alni min al-mutatahhireen (O Allah, make me of those who repent and make me of those who purify themselves)";

Using siwaak to cleanse and perfume the mouth that is going to recite Qur'an in a short while, because the Prophet (peace and blessings of Allah be upon him) said: "Purify your mouths for the Qur'an." (Reported by al-Bazzaar, who said: we do not have it with any better isnaad than this. Kashf al-Astaar, 1/242. Al-Haythami said: its men are thiqaat. 2/99. Al-Albaani said: its isnaad is jayyid. Al-Sahihah, 1213);

Wearing one's best and cleanest clothes, because Allah says (interpretation of the meaning): "O Children of Adam! Take your adornment (by wearing your clean clothes) while praying..." [Al-A'raaf 7:31]. Allah is most deserving of seeing us "take our adornment" for Him. Clean, pleasant smelling clothes are also more comfortable and relaxing, unlike clothes for sleeping or working in.

We should also prepare ourselves by covering our 'awrah properly, purifying the spot where we are going to pray, getting ready early and waiting for the prayer, and making the rows straight and solid, without any gaps, because the shayaateen come in through the gaps in the rows.

Moving at a measured pace during prayer

The Prophet (peace and blessings of Allah be upon him) used to move at a measured pace during salaah, allowing every bone to return to its place. (Its isnaad is classed as saheeh in Sifat al-Salaat, p. 134, 11th edn. Ibn Khuzaymah also classed it as saheeh as mentioned by al-Haafiz in al-Fath, 2/308). He commanded those who were not doing their prayer properly to do this too. He said, "None of you has prayed properly until he does this." (Reported by Abu Dawood, 1/536, no. 858).

Abu Qutaadah (may Allah be pleased with him) said: "The Prophet (peace and blessings of Allah be upon him) said: 'The worst type of thief is the one who steals from his prayer.' He said, 'O Messenger of Allah, how can a person steal from his prayer?' He said, 'By not doing rukoo' and sujood properly.'" (Reported by Ahmad and al-Haakim, 1/229; Saheeh al-Jaami', 997).

Abu 'Abd-Allaah al-Ash'ari (may Allah be pleased with him) said: "The Prophet (peace and blessings of Allah be upon him) said, 'The one who does not do rukoo' properly, and pecks in sujood, is like a starving man who eats only one or two dates; it does not do him any good at all.'" (Reported by al-Tabaraani in al-Kabeer, 4/115. In Saheeh al-Jaami' it says, hasan).

The one who does not move at a measured pace in his prayer cannot have khushoo' because haste is a barrier to khushoo' and pecking like a crow is a barrier to reward.

Remembering death whilst praying

The Prophet (peace and blessings of Allah be upon him) said: "Remember death in your prayer, for the man who remembers death during his prayer is bound to pray properly, and pray the prayer of a man who does not think that he will pray any other prayer." (al-Silsilat al-Sahihah by al-Albaani, 1421. It was reported from al-Suyooti that al-Haafiz ibn Hajar classed this hadith as hasan).

The Prophet (peace and blessings of Allah be upon him) also advised Abu Ayub (may Allah be pleased with him): "When you stand up to pray, pray a farewell prayer." (Reported by Ahmad, 5/412; Saheeh al-Jaami', no. 742) – meaning the prayer of one who thinks that he will not pray another prayer. The person who is praying will no doubt die, and there is some prayer that will be his last prayer, so let him have khushoo' in the prayer that he is doing, for he does not know whether this will be his last prayer.

Thinking about the aayaat and adhkaar being recited during the prayer and interacting with them

The Qur'an was revealed to be pondered over. Allah says (interpretation of the meaning): "(This is) a Book (the Qur'an) which We have sent down to you, full of blessings that they may ponder over its Verses, and that men of understanding may remember." [Saad 38:29]. No one can ponder over its verses unless he has some knowledge of the meaning of what he is reciting, so that he can think about it and be moved to tears by it. Allah says (interpretation of the meaning): "And those who, when they are reminded of the aayaat (proofs, evidences, verses, lessons, signs, revelations, etc.) of their Lord, fall not deaf and blind thereat." [al-Furqaan 25:73]. Thus the importance of studying Tafseer (Qur'an commentary) is quite clear. Ibn Jareer (may Allah have mercy on him) said: "I am astonished at people who read the Qur'an and do not know what it means. How can they enjoy reading it?" (Muqaddimat Tafseer al-Tabari by Mahmood Shaakir, 1/10. For this reason it is important for the reader of Qur'an to look at a Tafseer, even if it is abridged, when he is reading. For example, he could read Zubdat al-Tafseer by al-Ashqar, which is abridged from the Tafseer of al-Shawkaani, and the Tafseer of al-'Allaamah Ibn Sa'di, entitled Tayseer al-Kareem al-Rahmaan fi Tafseer Kalaam al-Mannaan. At the very least he could consult a book explaining the unusual words such as al-Mu'jam al-Jaami' li Ghareeb Mufradaat al-Qur'an by 'Abd al-'Azeez al-Seerwaan, which is a compilation of four books of unusual words used in the Qur'an).

Another way of helping oneself to ponder over the meanings is to repeat aayaat, because this will help one to think deeply and look again at the meanings. The Prophet (peace and blessings of Allah be upon him) used to do this. It was reported that he spent a night repeating one aayah until morning came. The aayah was (interpretation of the meaning): "If you punish them, they are Your slaves, and if You forgive them, verily You, only You are the All-Mighty, the All-Wise." [al-Maa'idah 5:118]. (Reported by Ibn Khuzaymah, 1/271 and Ahmad, 5/149; Sifat al-Salaah, p. 102). [Translator's note: Shaykh al-Albaani's book Sifat al-Salaah is available in English under the title The Prophet's Prayer described by Shaikh Muhammad Naasir-ud-Deen al-Albaani, translated by Usama ibn Suhaib Hasan, Al-Haneef Publications, Ipswich, UK, 1993]

Another way of helping oneself ponder over the meanings is to interact with the aayaat. Hudhayfah said: " I prayed with the Messenger of Allah (peace and blessings of Allah be upon him) one night... he was reciting at length. If he recited an aayah that mentioned tasbeeh, he would say Subhaan Allah; if it mentioned a question, he would ask a question; if it mentioned seeking refuge with Allah, he would seek refuge with Allah." (Reported by Muslim, no. 772). According to another report, [Hudhayfah] said: "I prayed with the Messenger of Allah (peace and blessings of Allah be upon him), and if he recited an aayah that mentioned mercy, he would ask for mercy; if he recited an aayah that mentioned punishment, he would seek refuge with Allah, and if he recited an aayah that mentioned deanthropomorphism of Allah, he would say Subhaan-Allah." (Ta'zeem Qadr al-Salaah, 1/327). This was reported concerning qiyaam al-layl (prayer at night).

One of the Sahaabah – Qutaadah ibn al-Nu'maan (may Allah be pleased with him) – prayed qiyaam at night and did not recite anything but Qul Huwa Allah Ahad, repeating it and not adding anything more. (Al-Bukhari, al-Fath, 9/59; Ahmad, 3/43)

Sa'eed ibn 'Ubayd al-Taa'i said: "I heard Sa'eed ibn Jubayr leading them in prayer during the month of Ramadan, and he was repeating this aayah (interpretation of the meaning): '... they will come to know, when iron collars will be rounded over their necks, and the chains, they shall be dragged along, in the boiling water, then they will be burned in the Fire.' [Ghaafir 40:70-72]." Al-Qaasim said: "I saw Sa'eed ibn Jubayr praying qiyaam al-layl and reciting (interpretation of the meaning): 'And be afraid of the Day when you shall be brought back to Allah. Then every person shall be paid what he earned...' [al-Baqarah 2:281], and repeating it twenty-odd times." A man of Qays who was known by the kunyah Abu 'Abd-Allaah said: "We stayed with al-Hasan one night, and he got up to pray qiyaam al-layl. He prayed and did not stop repeating this ayah until just before dawn (interpretation of the meaning): '... and if you count the Blessings of Allah, never will you be able to count them...' [Ibrahim 14:34]. When morning came, we said, 'O Abu Sa'eed, you did not recite any more than this one ayah all night.' He said, 'I learn a great deal from it: I do not glance at anything but I see a blessing in it, but what we do not know about Allah's blessings is far greater.'" (Al-Tidhkaar li'l-Qurtubi, p. 125).

Haroon ibn Rabaab al-Usaydi used to get up at night to pray Tahajjud, and he would repeat this ayah until daybreak (interpretation of the meaning): "... 'Would that we were but sent back (to the world)! Then we would not deny the aayaat (signs, verses) of our Lord, and we would be of the believers!'" [al-An'aam 6:27], and weeping until daybreak.

Another way of helping oneself to ponder over the meanings is to memorize Qur'an and various adhkaar to be recited during different parts of the prayer, so that one may recite them and think about their meanings.

There is no doubt that these actions – thinking about the meanings, repeating and interacting with the words – are among the greatest means of increasing khushoo', as Allah says (interpretation of the meaning): "And they fall down on their faces weeping and it adds to their humility [khushoo']'" [al-Isra' 17:109].

The following is a moving story that illustrates how the Prophet (peace and blessings of Allah be upon him) had khushoo', as well as explaining how it is obligatory to think of the meaning of the aayaat. 'Ataa' said: " 'Ubayd ibn 'Umayr and I entered upon

'Aa'ishah (may Allah be pleased with her) and Ibn 'Umayr said to her, 'Tell us of the most amazing thing you saw on the part of the Messenger of Allah (peace and blessings of Allah be upon him).' She wept and said, 'He got up one night and said, "O 'Aa'ishah, leave me to worship my Lord." I said, "By Allah, I love to be close to you, and I love what makes you happy." So he got up and purified himself, then he stood and prayed. He kept weeping until his lap got wet, then he wept and kept weeping until the floor got wet. Bilaal came to tell him that it was time to pray, and when he saw him weeping, he said, "O Messenger of Allah, you are weeping when Allah has forgiven you all your past and future sins?" He said, "Should I not be a grateful slave? Tonight some aayaat have been revealed to me; woe to the one who recites them and does not think about what is in them (**interpretation of the meaning**): 'Verily! In the creation of the heavens and the earth…'" [Aal 'Imraan 3:190… or al-Baqarah 2:164].'" (Reported by Ibn Hibaan. He said in al-Silsilat al-Sahihah, no. 68: this is a jayyid isnaad).

One example of interacting with the aayaat is to say "Aameen" after al-Faatihah, which brings a great reward. The Messenger of Allah (peace and blessings of Allah be upon him) said: "If the imaam says 'Aameen,' then say 'Aameen' too, for whoever says 'Aameen' and it coincides with the 'Aameen' of the angels, will have all his previous sins forgiven." (Reported by al-Bukhari, no. 747). Another example is responding to the imaam when he says "Sami' Allaahu liman hamidah (Allah hears the one who praises Him)"; the members of the congregation should say, "Rabbanaa wa laka'l-hamd (O our Lord, to You be praise)." This also brings a great reward. Rifaa'ah ibn Raafi' al-Zirqi said: "One day we were praying behind the Prophet (peace and blessings of Allah be upon him). When he raised his head, he said, 'Sami' Allaahu liman hamidah,' and a man behind him said, 'Rabbanaa wa laka'l-hamdu hamdan katheeran tayyiban mubaarakan fih (Our Lord to You be much good and blessed praise).' When he finished, he said, 'Who is the one who spoke?' The man said, 'Me.' He said, 'I saw thirty-odd angels rushing to see who would write it down first.'" (Reported by al-Bukhari, al-Fath, 2/284).

Pausing at the end of each ayah

This is more helpful in understanding and thinking about the meaning, and it is the Sunnah of the Prophet (peace and blessings of Allah be upon him), as Umm Salamah (may Allah be pleased with her) described how the Messenger of Allah (peace and blessings of Allah be upon him) would recite, "Bismillah il-Rahmaan il-Raheem", and according to one report, he would pause, then say, "Al-hamdu Lillaahi Rabbi'l-'Aalameen, al-Rahmaan, al-Raheem." Then according to one report, he would pause, then say, "Maaliki yawm il-deen," and he would break up his recitation ayah by ayah. (Reported by Abu Dawood, no. 4001; classed as Saheeh by al-Albaani in al-Irwaa', where its isnaads are described. 2/60).

Pausing at the end of each ayah is Sunnah even if the meaning continues into the next ayah.

Reciting in slow, rhythmic tones (tarteel) and making one's voice beautiful when reciting

As Allah says (interpretation of the meaning): "... and recite the Qur'an (aloud) in a slow, (pleasant tone and) style." [al-Muzzammil 73:4]. The recitation of the Prophet (peace and blessings of Allah be upon him) was clear, with each letter pronounced distinctly." (Musnad Ahmad, 6/294, with a saheeh isnaad. Sifat al-Salaah, p. 105).

The Prophet (peace and blessings of Allah be upon him) "would recite a surah in such slow rhythmic tones that it would be longer than would seem possible." **(Reported by Muslim, no. 733).**

This slow, measured pace of recitation is more conducive to reflection and khushoo' than a hurried, hasty reading.

Another way of helping oneself to have khushoo' is by making one's voice beautiful when reciting. This is something that was advised by the Prophet (peace and blessings of Allah be upon him), as when he said, "Beautify the Qur'an with your voices, for a fine voice increases the Qur'an in beauty." (Reported by al-Haakim, 1/575; Saheeh al-Jaami', no. 3581).

Beautifying it with one's voice does not mean elongating the vowels and giving it a tune in the manner of corrupt people; it means beautifying one's voice with the fear of Allah, as the Prophet (peace and blessings of Allah be upon him) said: "Truly, the one who has one of the finest voices among the people for reciting the Qur'an is the one whom you think fears Allah when you hear him recite." (Reported by Ibn Maajah, 1/1339; Saheeh al-Jaami', no. 2202).

Knowing that Allah responds to prayers

The Prophet (peace and blessings of Allah be upon him) said: "Allah, the Blessed and Exalted has said: 'I have divided the prayer between Myself and My slave, into two halves, and My slave shall have what he has asked for.' When the slave says 'Praise be to Allah, Lord of the Worlds,' Allah says, 'My slave has praised Me.' When the slave says, 'The Most Merciful, the Bestower of Mercy,' Allah says, 'My slave has extolled me.' When the slave says, 'Master of the Day of Judgement,' Allah says, 'My slave has glorified me.' When the slave says, 'It is You alone we worship and it is You alone we ask for help,' Allah says, 'This is between Me and My slave, and My slave shall have what he asked for.' When the slave says, 'Guide us to the Straight Path, the path of those whom You have favoured, not the path of those who receive Your anger, nor of those who go astray,' Allah says, 'All these are for My slave, and My slave shall have what he asked for.'" (Saheeh Muslim, Kitaab al-Salaah, Baab wujoob qiraa'at al-Faatihah fi kulli rak'ah). [Words in italics are the translation of the meaning of Soorat al-Faatihah – Translator].

This is a great and important hadith. If everyone kept it in mind when he prays, he would attain immense khushoo' and al-Faatihah would have a great impact on him. How could it be otherwise, when he feels that his Lord is addressing him and giving him what he is asking for?

This "conversation" with Allah must be respected and accorded its proper value. The Messenger of Allah (peace and blessings of Allah be upon him) said: "When any one of you stands to pray, he is conversing with his Lord, so let him pay attention to how he speaks to Him." (al-Haakim, al-Mustadrak, 1/236; Saheeh al-Jaami', 1538).

Praying with a barrier (sutrah) in front of one and praying close to it

Another thing that will help one to have khushoo' is paying attention to the matter of having a sutrah and praying close to it, because this will restrict your field of vision, protect you from the Shaytan and keep people from passing in front of you, which causes a distraction and reduces the reward of the prayer.

The Prophet (peace and blessings of Allah be upon him) said: "When any one of you prays, let him pray facing a sutrah, and let him get close to it." (Reported by Abu Dawood, no. 695, 1/446; Saheeh al-Jaami', no. 651).

Getting close to the sutrah is very beneficial, as the Prophet (peace and blessings of Allah be upon him) said: "When any one of you prays facing a sutrah, let him get close to it so that the Shaytan cannot interrupt his prayer." (Reported by Abu Dawood, no. 695, 1/446; Saheeh al-Jaami', no. 650).

The Sunnah in getting close to the sutrah is to have three cubits between it and the spot where one prostrates, or to allow enough space for a sheep to pass between the two, as is reported in the Saheeh ahadith. (Al-Bukhari; see al-Fath, 1/574, 579).

The Prophet (peace and blessings of Allah be upon him) advised the one who is praying not to allow anyone to pass between him and his sutrah. He said: "When any one of you is praying, he should not allow anyone to pass in front of him, and he should prevent him as most as he can. If he insists, he should fight him, for he has a companion [i.e., Shaytan] with him." (Reported by Muslim, 1/260; Saheeh al-Jaami', no. 755).

Al-Nawawi (may Allah have mercy on him) said: "The wisdom in using a sutrah is to lower your gaze and not to look beyond it, and to prevent anyone from passing in front of you... and to prevent the Shaytan from passing in front of you and trying to corrupt your prayer." (Sharh Saheeh Muslim, 4/216).

Placing the right hand on the left hand on the chest

The Prophet (peace and blessings of Allah be upon him), when he stood up to pray, used to place his right hand on his left hand (Muslim, no. 401), and place them on his chest (Abu Dawood, no. 759; see also Irwa' al-Ghaleel, 2/71). The Messenger of Allah (peace and blessings of Allah be upon him) said, "We Prophets were commanded... to place our right hands on our left hands in prayer." (Reported by al-Tabaraani in al-Mu'jam al-Kabeer, no. 11485. Al-Haythami said: Al-Tabaraani reported it in al-Awsat and its men are the men of saheeh. Al-Majma', 3/155).

Imam Ahmad (may Allah have mercy on him) was asked about the meaning of placing one hand on top of the other when standing in prayer. He said: "It is humility before the Almighty." (Al-Khushoo' fi'l-Salaah by Ibn Rajab, p. 21).

Ibn Hajar (may Allah have mercy on him) said: "The 'ulamaa' said: the meaning of this posture is that it is the attitude of the humble petitioner, it is more likely to prevent fidgeting, and it is more conducive to khushoo'." (Fath al-Baari, 2/224).

Looking at the place of prostration

It was reported from 'Aa'ishah that "the Messenger of Allah (peace and blessings of Allah be upon him) used to pray with his head tilted forward and his gaze lowered, looking at the ground." (Reported by al-Haakim, 1/479. He said it is saheeh according to the condition of the two Shaykhs [al-Bukhari and Muslim], and al-Albaani agreed with him in Sifat al-Salaah, p. 89).

When the Prophet (peace and blessings of Allah be upon him) entered the Ka'bah, his eyes never left the place of his prostration until he came out again. (Reported by al-Haakim in al-Mustadrak, 1/479. He said it is saheeh according to the condition of the two shaykhs, and al-Dhahabi agreed with him. Al-Albaani said, It is as they said. Irwaa' al-Ghaleel, 2/73).

When a person sits for Tashahhud, he should look at the finger with which he is pointing as he is moving it, as it was reported that the Prophet (peace and blessings of Allah be upon him) "would point with the finger next to the thumb towards the qiblah, and focus his gaze upon it." (Reported by Ibn Khuzaymah, 1/355, no. 719. The editor said: its isnaad is saheeh. See Sifat al-Salaah, p. 139). According to another report he "pointed with his index finger and did not allow his gaze to wander beyond it." (Reported by Ahmad, 4/3, and by Abu Dawood, no. 990)

Note

There is a question in the minds of some people who pray, which is: what is the ruling on closing the eyes during prayer, especially when a person feels that this increases his khushoo'?

The answer is that this goes against the Sunnah that was reported from the Prophet (peace and blessings of Allah be upon him) that was just referred to above. Closing the eyes means that a person misses out on the Sunnah of looking at the place of prostration and at his finger. But there is more to the matter than this, so we should listen to the opinion of an expert, al-'Allaamah Abu 'Abd-Allah Ibn al-Qayyim, which will explain the matter further. He (may Allah have mercy on him) said: "It is not part of the Prophet's teaching to close the eyes during prayer. We have already mentioned how he used to look at his finger during the Tashahhud and the du'a', and he would not let his gaze wander beyond his finger... Another indication [of the fact that he kept his eyes open] is the fact that he stretched his hand forth to take the bunch of grapes when he saw Paradise, and he also saw Hell and the woman (who had tormented) the cat, and the owner of Stick (al-Mihjan). Likewise, he pushed away the animal that wanted to pass in front of him whilst he was praying, and he pushed back the boy, and the young girl, and the two young girls. He used to wave to those whom he saw greeting him (whilst he was praying). There is also a hadith that describes how the Shaytan tried to tempt him whilst he was praying, so he grabbed him and strangled him, as he had seen him with his own eyes. From these ahadith and others we learn that he did not close his eyes when he prayed.

The fuqahaa' differ as to whether closing the eyes during prayer is makrooh. Imaam Ahmad and others did count it as makrooh, and said: "This is the action of the Jews," but others allowed it and did not count it as makrooh. The correct view is that if keeping the eyes open does not affect a person's khushoo', then this is better, but if keeping the eyes open affects a person's khushoo because of decorations, adornments etc. in front of him, which distract him, then it is not makrooh at all for him to close his eyes. The opinion that indeed it is mustahabb in this case is closer to the principles and aims of sharee'ah than saying it is makrooh. And Allah knows best. (Zaad al-Ma'aad, 1/293, Daar al-Risaalah edn.)

Thus it is clear that the Sunnah is not to close one's eyes, unless it is necessary to do so in order to avoid something that may adversely affect one's khushoo'.

Moving the index finger

This is something which is neglected by many worshippers because they are ignorant of its great benefits and its effect on khushoo'.

The Prophet (peace and blessings of Allah be upon him) said: "It is more powerful against the Shaytan than iron" (reported by Imaam Ahmad, 2/119, with a hasan isnaad, as stated in Sifat al-Salaah, p. 159), i.e., pointing with the forefinger during the Tashahhud is more painful to the Shaytan than being beaten with a rod of iron, because it reminds the slave of the Unity of Allah and to be sincere in his worship of Him alone, and this is what the Shaytan hates most; we seek refuge with Allah from him." (al-Fath al-Rabbani by al-Saa'idi, 4/15).

Because of this great benefit, the Sahaabah, may Allah be pleased with them, used to enjoin one another to do this and were very keen to remember to do this thing which so many people nowadays take so lightly. It was reported that "the Companions of the Prophet (peace and blessings of Allah be upon him) used to enjoin one another, i.e., with regard to pointing with the finger during the du'a'." (Reported by Ibn Abi Shaybah with a hasan isnaad, as stated in Sifat al-Salaah, p. 141. See al-Musannaf, no. 9732, part 10, page 381, Dar al-Salafiyyah, India, edn.)

The Sunnah in pointing with the forefinger is that it should remain raised and moving, pointing towards the qiblah, throughout the Tashahhud.

Varying the soorahs, aayaat, adhkaar and du'aa's recited in prayer

This makes the worshipper feel that he is encountering new meanings and moving between different topics mentioned in the aayaat and adhkaar. This is what a person misses out on if he only memorizes a few soorahs (especially the short ones) and adhkaar. Varying what one recites is the Sunnah and is more conducive to khushoo'.

If we study what the Prophet (peace and blessings of Allah of upon him) used to recite in his prayer, we will see this variation. For example, with regard to the opening du'a', we find examples such as the following:

"Allaahumma baa'id bayni wa bayna khataayaaya kamaa baa'adta bayn al-mashriqi wa'l-maghrib. Allaahumma naqqani min khataayaaya kamaa yunaqqaa al-thawb al-abyad min al-danas. Allaahumma'ghsilni min khataayaaya bi'l-maa' wa'l-thalj wa'l-barad (O Allah, separate me (far) from my sins as You have separated (far) the East from the West. O Allah, cleanse me of my sins as white cloth is cleansed from dirt. O Allah, wash me of my sins with water, snow and ice)."

"Wajahtu wajhi li'lladhi fatara al-samawaati wa'l-ard haneefan, wa maa ana min al-mushrikeen. Inna salaati wa nusuki wa mahyaaya wa mamaati Lillaahi Rabb il - 'aalameen, laa shareeka lahu wa bidhaalika umirtu wa ana awwal al-muslimeen (I have set my face towards the Originator of the heavens and the earth sincerely and I am not among the mushrikeen. Indeed my prayer, my sacrifice, my living and my dying are for Allah, the Lord of the Worlds: no partner has He. With this I have been commanded, and I am the first of the Muslims (those who submit to Him)."

"Subhaanak Allaahumma wa bi hamdika wa tabaaraka ismuka wa ta'aala jadduka wa laa ilaaha ghayruk (Glory and praise be to You, O Allah, blessed be Your name and exalted be Your majesty. There is no god besides You)."

And other du'aa's and adhkaar which the worshipper can use at various times.

Among the soorahs which the Prophet (peace and blessings of Allah of upon him) used to recite during Salaat al-Fajr we find a great and blessed number.

The longer mufassal soorahs (soorahs from the last seventh of the Qur'an), such as al-Waaqi'ah [56], al-Toor [52] and Qaaf [50], and shorter mufassal soorahs such as Idhaa al-shamsu kuwwirat [al-Takweer 81], al-Zalzalah [99], and al-Mi'wadhatayn [the last two soorahs].

It was reported that he recited al-Room [30], Yaa-Seen [36] and al-Saaffaat [37], and on Fridays he would recite al-Sajah [32] and al-Insaan [76, a.k.a. al-Dhahr] in Fajr prayer.

It was reported that in Salaat al-Zuhr, he would recite the equivalent of thirty aayaat in each of the two rak'ahs, and that he recited al-Taariq [86], al-Burooj [85] and wa'l-layli idhaa yaghshaa [al-Layl, 92].

In Salaat al-'Asr, he would recite the equivalent of fifteen aayaat in each rak'ah, and he would recite the soorahs already mentioned in connection with Salaat al-Zuhr.

In Salaat al-Maghrib, he would recite short mufassal soorahs such as al-teeni wa'l-zaytoon [al-Teen 95], and he recited Soorat Muhammad [47], al-Toor [52], al-Mursalaat [77] and others.

In 'Ishaa' he would recite medium-length mufassal soorahs, such as al-shamsu wa duhaahaa [al-Shams 91], idhaa'l-samaa'u inshaqqat [al-Inshiqaaq 84]. He told Mu'aadh to recite al-A'laa [87], al-Qalam [68] and al-layli idhaa yaghshaa [al-Layl, 92].

In qiyaam al-layl, he used to recite the long soorahs. It was reported that he (peace and blessings of Allah be upon him) used to recite 200 or 150 aayaat, and sometimes he used to shorten the recitation.

He used to vary the adhkaar he recited in rukoo'. In addition to "Subhaana Rabbi al-'Azeem (Glory be to my Supreme Lord)" and "Subhaana Rabbi al-'Azeem wa bi hamdih (Glory and praise be to my Supreme Lord)", he would say: "Subbooh, Quddoos, Rabb il-Malaa'ikati wa'l-Rooh (Perfect, Blessed, Lord of the Angels and the Spirit)," or, "Allaahumma laka raka'tu wa bika aamantu wa laka aslamtu wa 'alayka tawakkaltu anta Rabbi. Khasha'a sam'i wa basari wa dammi wa lahmi wa 'azmi wa 'asabi Lillaahi Rabbi'l-'Alaameen (O Allah, to You have I bowed, to You I have submitted, in You I have believed, to You I have submitted and in You I have put my trust. Humbled are my hearing, my seeing, my blood, my flesh, my bones and my nerves for Allah, Lord of the Worlds)."

When standing upright from rukoo', after saying "Sami'a Allah liman hamidah (Allah listens to the one who praises Him)" he would say, "Rabbanaa wa laka'l-hamd (Our Lord, and to You be all praise)," or sometimes, "Rabbanaa laka'l-hamd (Our Lord, to You be all praise)," or, "Allaahumma Rabbanaa [wa] laka'l-hamd (O Allah our Lord, [and] to You be all praise)." Sometimes he would add the words: "Mil'a al-samawaati wa mil'a al-ard wa mil'a maa shi'ta min shay'in ba'd ([Praise] filling the heavens, filling the earth, and filling whatever else You wish)", and sometimes he would add, "Ahl al-thanaa'i wa'l-majd, laa maani'a limaa a'tayta wa laa mu'tiya limaa mana't, wa laa yanfa'u dhaa'l-jaddi minka'l-jadd (Lord of Glory and Majesty! None can withhold what You grant, and none can grant what You withhold; nor can the possessions of an owner benefit him in front of You)."

In sujood, in addition to "Subhaan Rabbi al-A'laa (Glory be to my Lord Most High)" and "Subhaana Rabbi al-A'laa wa bi hamdih (Glory and praise be to my Lord Most High)," he would say "Subbooh, Quddoos, Rabb il-Malaa'ikati wa'l-Rooh (Perfect, Blessed, Lord of the Angels and the Spirit)," or "Subhaanak Allaahumma Rabbanaa wa bi hamdik, Allaahumma'ghfir li (Glory and raise be to you O Allah, our Lord. O Allah forgive me)" or "Allaahumma laka sajadtu wa bika aamantu wa laka aslamtu, sajada wajhi lilladhi khalaqahu wa sawwarahu wa shaqqa sam'ahu wa basarahu, tabaarak Allaahu ahsaan al-khaaliqeen (O Allah, to You I have prostrated, in You I have believed and to You I have submitted. My face has prostrated to the One Who created it and gave it shape, then brought forth its hearing and its vision. Blessed be Allah, the Best to create)," and others.

When sitting between the two prostrations, in addition to "Rabb ighfir li, Rabb ighfir li (Lord, forgive me, Lord, forgive me)," he would say, "Allaahumm aghfir li warhamni wajbarni wa arfa'ni wahdini wa 'aafini wa arzuqni (O Allah, forgive me, have mercy on me, strengthen me, raise my rank, guide me, pardon me, sustain me)."

A number of versions of the tashahhud have been narrated, such as: "Al-tahiyyaatu Lillaahi wa'l-salawaatu wa'l-tayyibaat al-salaamu 'alayka ayyuha'l-Nabiyyu ...etc. (All compliments, prayers and pure words are due to Allah. Peace be upon you, O

Prophet...)" and "Al-Tahiyyaat al-mubaarakaat al-salawaat al-tayyibaatu Lillaahi, al-salaamu 'alayka ayyuha'l-Nabiyyu...etc. (All compliments, blessed words, prayers, pure words are due to Allah. Peace be upon you, O Prophet...)" and "Al-tahiyyaat al-tayyibaat al-salawaatu Lillaahi, al-salaamu 'alayka ayyuha'l-Nabiyyu... etc. (All compliments, good words and prayers are due to Allah. Peace be upon you, O Prophet ...)."

So the worshipper may use one form one time and another at another time, and so on.

There are a number of versions of the prayers sent upon the Prophet (peace and blessings of Allah be upon him), such as:

"Allaahumma salli 'ala Muhammad wa 'ala aali Muhammad kamaa salayta 'ala Ibrahim wa 'ala aali Ibrahim, innaka Hameedun Majeed. Allaahumma baarik 'ala Muhammadin wa 'ala aali Muhammadin kamaa baarakta 'ala Ibrahim wa 'ala aali Ibrahim innaka Hameedun Majeed (O Allah, send prayers on Muhammad and on the family of Muhammad, as You sent prayers on Ibrahim and the family of Ibrahim, verily You are Worthy of Praise and Full of Glory; O Allah, send blessings on Muhammad and on the family of Muhammad, as You sent blessings on Ibrahim and the family of Ibrahim, verily You are Worthy of Praise and Full of Glory)."

Or:

"Allaahumma salli 'ala Muhammad wa 'ala aali baytihi wa 'ala azwaajihi wa dhuriyatihi kamaa salayta 'ala aali Ibrahim, innaka Hameedun Majeed wa baarik 'ala Muhammadin wa 'ala aali baytihi wa 'ala azwaajihi wa dhuriyatihi kamaa baarakta 'ala aali Ibrahim innaka Hameedun Majeed (O Allah, send prayers on Muhammad and on his family, wives and progeny, as You sent prayers on the family of Ibrahim, verily You are Worthy of Praise and Full of Glory; O Allah, send blessings on Muhammad and on his family, wives and progeny, as You sent blessings on the family of Ibrahim, verily You are Worthy of Praise and Full of Glory)."

Or:

"Allaahumma salli 'ala Muhammad al-Nabiyy al-Ummi wa 'ala aali Muhammad kamaa salayta 'ala aali Ibrahim, wa baarik 'ala Muhammad al-Nabiyy al-Ummi wa 'ala aali Muhammadin kamaa baarakta 'ala aali Ibrahim fi'l-'aalameen, innaka Hameedun Majeed (O Allah, send prayers on Muhammad the Unlettered Prophet and on the family of Muhammad, as You sent prayers on the family of Ibrahim, and send blessings on Muhammad the Unlettered Prophet and on the family of Muhammad, as You sent blessings on the family of Ibrahim among the nations, verily You are Worthy of Praise and Full of Glory)."

Other similar versions have also been narrated, and the Sunnah is to vary among them, as stated above. There is nothing wrong with reciting one version more than others, because it is more strongly proven and better known in the books of saheeh ahaadeeth, or because the Prophet (peace and blessings of Allah be upon him) taught one version rather than others to his Sahaabah when they asked him about it, and so on.

(All of the above texts etc. have been taken from Sifat al-Salaat al-Nabi (peace and blessings of Allah be upon him) by Shaykh Muhammad Naasir al-Deen al-Albaani, which he compiled from the books of hadeeth).

Performing sujood al-tilaawah when reciting an ayah where this is required

One of the etiquettes of reciting Qur'an is to perform sujood al-tilaawah (prostration for recitation) when one recites an ayah containing a "sajdah" (place where a prostration is required). In His Book, Allah describes the Prophets and the righteous as follows (interpretation of the meaning): *"... When the Verses of the Most Beneficent were recited unto them, they fell down prostrating and weeping."* **[Maryam 19:58]**. Ibn Katheer (may Allah have mercy on him) said: *"The scholars agreed that we should prostrate here [when reciting this ayah] so as to follow their example."* **(Tafseer al-Qur'an al-'Azeem, 5/238, Daar al-Sha'b edn.)**

Sujood al-Tilaawah in prayer is very important because it increases khushoo'. Allah says (interpretation of the meaning): *"And they fall down on their faces weeping and it adds to their humility [khushoo']."* **[al-Israa' 17:109]**.

It was reported that the Prophet (peace and blessings of Allah be upon him) prostrated when he recited Soorat al-Najm [53] in his prayer. Al-Bukhari (may Allah have mercy on him) reported in his Saheeh that Abu Raafi' said: *"I prayed 'Ishaa' with Abu Hurayrah (may Allah be pleased with him) and he recited Idhaa al-samaa'u inshaqqat [al-Inshiqaaq 84] and prostrated. I asked him about it, and he said, 'I prostrated behind Abu'l-Qaasim [the Prophet] (peace and blessings of Allah be upon him), and I will continue to do so until I meet him again."* **(Saheeh al-Bukhari, Kitaab al-Adhaan, Baab al-Jahr bi'l-'Ishaa').**

It is important to maintain the practice of sujood al-tilaawah, especially since it causes annoyance to the Shaytan and suppresses him, thus weakening his hold on the worshipper. Abu Hurayrah said: *"The Messenger of Allah (peace and blessings of Allah be upon him) said: 'When the son of Adam recites a sajdah, the Shaytan goes away weeping, saying, "Woe to him! He was commanded to prostrate and he prostrated, so Paradise is his; I was ordered to prostrate and I disobeyed, so Hell is my fate!"'"* **(Reported by Imaam Muslim in his Saheeh, no. 133).**

Seeking refuge with Allah from the Shaytan

The Shaytan is our enemy, and one of the aspects of his enmity is his whispering insinuating thoughts (waswaas) to the worshipper at prayer so as to take away his khushoo' and confuse him in his prayer.

Waswaas is a problem that befalls everyone who turns to Allah with dhikr and other kinds of worship; it is inevitable, so one has to stand firm and be patient, and persist in the dhikr or salaah, and not give up. His sticking to it will ward off the Shaytaan's plots from himself. "... Ever feeble indeed is the plot of Shaytan." [al-Nisaa' 4:76 - interpretation of the meaning].

Every time the slave wants to turn his thoughts towards Allah, thoughts of other matters come sneaking into his mind. The Shaytan is like a bandit lying in wait to launch an ambush: every time the slave wants to travel towards Allah, the Shaytan wants to cut off his route. For this reason, it was said to one of the salaf: "The Jews and Christians say that they do not suffer from the problem of waswaas." He said, "They are speaking the truth, for what would the Shaytan want with a house that is in ruins?" (Majma' al-Fataawa, 22/608).

This is a good analogy. It is as if there are three houses: the house of a king, filled with his treasure and savings, the house of a slave, containing his treasure and savings, and an empty house with nothing in it. If a thief comes to steal from one of the three houses, which one will he choose? (al-Waabil al-Sayib, p. 43).

When the slave stands up to pray, the Shaytan feels jealous of him, because he is standing in the greatest position, one that is closest [to Allah] and most annoying and grievous to the Shaytan. So he tries to stop him from establishing prayer in the first place, then he continues trying to entice him and make him forget, and "making assaults on him with his cavalry and infantry" [cf. Al-Isra' 17:64], until he thinks of prayer as less important, so he starts to neglect it, and eventually gives it up altogether. If the Shaytan fails to achieve this, and the person ignores him and starts to pray, the enemy of Allah will come and try to distract him, by reminding him of things that he did not remember or think of before he started praying. A person may have forgotten about something altogether, but the Shaytan will remind him of it when he starts praying, so as to distract him from his prayers and take him away from Allah, so that his heart will no longer be in his prayers, and he will lose out on the honour and reward of Allah turning toward him, which is only attained by the one whose heart is really in his prayer. Thus he will finish his prayer no better off than when he started, with his burden of sins not reduced at all by his salaah, because prayer only expiates for sins when it is done properly, with perfect khushoo', and the person stands before Allah in body and soul." (Al-Waabil al-Sayib, p. 36).

The Prophet (peace and blessings of Allah be upon him) taught us the following methods of combatting the wiles of Shaytan and getting rid of his waswaas:

Abu'l-'Aas (may Allah be pleased with him) reported that he said, "O Messenger of Allah, the Shaytan interrupts me when I pray, and I get confused in my recitation." The Messenger of Allah (peace and blessings of Allah be upon him) said, "That is a Shaytan whose name is Khanzab. If you sense his presence, seek refuge with Allah from him, and spit [dry spitting] towards your left three times." [Abu'l-'Aas] said: "I did that and Allah took him away from me." (Reported by Muslim, no. 2203)

The Prophet (peace and blessings of Allah be upon him) also told us about another of the Shaytaan's tricks and how to deal with it. He said, "When any one of you gets up to pray, the Shaytan comes and confuses him – i.e., mixes up his prayer and creates doubts in his mind – so that he does not know how many [rak'ahs] he has prayed. If any one of you experiences that, he should do two prostrations whilst he is sitting." (Reported by al-Bukhari, Kitaab al-Sahw, Baab al-Sahw fi'l-Fard wa'l-Tatawwu').

Another of the Shaytaan's tricks was described as follows. The Prophet (peace and blessings of Allah be upon him) said: "If any one of you is praying and feels some movement in his back passage, and is uncertain as to whether he has broken his wudoo' or not, he should not end his prayer unless he hears a sound or smells an odour."

Indeed, his tricks may be very strange indeed, as the following hadith makes clear. Ibn 'Abbaas reported that the Prophet (peace and blessings of Allah be upon him) was asked about a man who thought that he had broken his wudoo' when he had not done so. The Messenger of Allah (peace and blessings of Allah be upon him) said: "The Shaytan may come to any one of you when he is praying and open his buttocks and make him think that he has broken his wudoo when in fact he has not. So if this happens to any one of you, let him not end his prayer unless he hears the sound of it with his ears or smells the odour of it with his nose." (Reported by al-Tabaraani in al-Kabeer, no.11556, part 11, p. 222. He said in Majma' al-Zawaa'id, 1/242, its men are the men of Saheeh).

Note

There is a devilish trick which "Khanzab" plays on some worshippers:

He tries to distract them by making them think of acts of worship other than the prayer that they are performing, by making them think of some issues of da'wah or knowledge, so that they start to think deeply about those matters and stop focusing on the prayer they are performing. He even confuses some of them by suggesting to them that 'Umar used to make plans for the army whilst he was praying. We should let Shaykh al-Islam Ibn Taymiyah explain this matter and set the record straight:

"With regard to what was reported, that 'Umar ibn al-Khattaab said, "I make plans for the army whilst I am praying," this was because 'Umar was commanded to engage in jihaad and he was the leader of the believers (ameer al-mu'mineen, i.e., the khaleefah), so he was also the leader of jihad. So in some respects he was like the one who prays the prayer of fear (salaat al-khawf) whilst also watching out for the enemy, whether or not there is actual fighting. He was commanded to pray, and also to engage in jihad, so he had to carry out both duties as much as he could. Allah says (interpretation of the meaning): 'O you who believe! When you meet (an enemy) force, take a firm stand against them and remember the Name of Allah much, so that you may be successful.' [al-Anfaal 8:45]. It is known that one cannot achieve the same peace of mind during jihad as at times of peace and security, so if it happens that a person's prayer is lacking because of jihad, this does not mean that his faith is lacking.

For this reason, standards may be regarded as being slightly relaxed in the case of prayer at times of danger as compared with times of peace. With regard to prayer at times of danger, Allah says (interpretation of the meaning): '… but when you are free from danger, perform al-salaah. Verily, the prayer is enjoined on the believers at fixed hours.' [al-Nisa' 4:103]. So the one who is commanded to establish prayer at times of peace is not commanded to do so in the same manner at times of danger.

Moreover, people are of varying levels in this regard. If a person's faith is strong, he will have the proper presence of mind when he prays, even if he thinks of other matters. Allah had caused the truth to reside firmly in 'Umar's heart, and he was al-muhaddith al-mulham ('the inspired speaker'), so there is nothing strange in a person of his calibre making plans for the army whilst performing the prayer. He was able to do this, whilst others are not, but undoubtedly when he did not have these concerns to think about, his presence of mind in prayer would be greater. And no doubt the prayer of the Prophet (peace and blessings of Allah be upon him) at times of safety was even more perfect that at times of danger, in terms of external appearance. If Allah has made allowances with regard to some of the external movements of the prayer at times of fear, how then about the internal aspects?

In conclusion, therefore, if a person who is pressed for time thinks about some obligatory matter whilst he is praying, this is not the same as a person who is not pressed for time thinking during prayer about some matter that is not obligatory. It may be that 'Umar could not give thought to making plans for the army except at that time, because he was the leader of the ummah with many obligations and responsibilities. Anyone could find himself in a similar situation, according to his position. People always think during prayer about things that they do not think of at other times, and some of this could come from the Shaytan. A man told one of the salaf that he had buried some money, but he had forgotten where he had buried it. He told him, 'Go and pray,' so he went and prayed, and he remembered where it was. It was said [to the salafi], 'How did you know that?' He said, 'I know that the Shaytan will not leave him alone when he prays without reminding him of something that matters to him, and there is nothing more important to this man than remembering where he had buried his money.' But the good slave will strive to attain perfect presence of mind in prayer, just as he strives to do everything else properly that he is commanded to do. And there is no help and no strength except in Allah, the Most High, the Almighty."

(Majmoo' al-Fataawa, 22/610)

Thinking of how the salaf were when they prayed

This will increase one's khushoo' and motivate one to follow their example. "If you were to see one of them when he stood up to pray and started reciting the words of his Master, it would cross his mind that he was standing before the Lord of the Worlds, so he would be filled with overwhelming awe." (Al-Khushoo' fi'l-Salaah by Ibn Rajab, p. 22).

Mujaahid (may Allah have mercy on him) said: "When one of them stood in prayer, he would be too fearful of his Lord to allow his eyes to be drawn to anything, or to turn aside or to fidget by playing with pebbles or anything else or to think of any worldly matter, unless he forgot, during prayer." (Ta'zeem Qadr al-Salaah, 1/188)

When Ibn al-Zubayr stood up to pray, he would be like a stick (i.e., immobile) with khushoo'. Once he was prostrating when a missile from a catapult was launched at him, when Makkah was being besieged, and part of his garment was torn away whilst he was praying, and he did not even raise his head. Muslimah ibn Bashshaar was praying in the mosque when part of it collapsed, and the people got up [and fled], but he was praying and did not even notice. We have heard that one of them was like a garment thrown on the floor; one of them would end his prayer with the colour of his complexion changed because he had been standing before Allah. One of them would not know who was standing to his right or left when he prayed. One of them would go pale when he did wudoo' for prayer, and it was said to him, "We see that when you do wudoo' a change comes over you." He said, "I know before Whom I am going to stand." When the time for prayer came, 'Ali ibn Abi Taalib would be visibly shaken, and the colour of his face would change. It was said to him, "What is the matter with you?' He said, "By Allah, there has come the time of the amaanah (trust) which Allah offered to the heavens and the earth, and the mountains, but they declined to bear it and were afraid of it, but I bore it [cf. Al-Ahzaab 33:72]." When Sa'eed al-Tanookhi prayed, there would be tears rolling down his cheeks onto his beard. We heard that one of the Taabi'een, when he stood up to pray, his colour would change, and he would say, "Do you know before Whom I am going to stand and with Whom I am going to talk?" Who among you has fear and respect like this? (Silaah al-Yaqazaan li Tard al-Shaytan, 'Abd al-'Azeez Sultaan, p. 209)

They said to 'Aamir ibn 'Abd al-Qays, "Do you think to yourself during prayer?" He said, "Is there anything I like to think about more than the prayer?" They said, "We think to ourselves during prayer." He said, "About Paradise and al-hoor ("houris") and so on?" They said, "No; about our families and our wealth." He said, "If I were to be run through with spears, it would be dearer to me than thinking to myself about worldly matters during prayer."

Sa'd ibn Mu'aadh said: "I have three qualities, which I wish I could keep up all the time, then I would really be something. When I am praying, I do not think about anything except the prayer I am doing; if I hear any hadith from the Messenger of Allah (peace and blessings of Allah be upon him), I do not have any doubts about it; and when I attend a janaazah (funeral), I do not think about anything except what the janaazah says and what is said to it." (Al-Fataawa li Ibn Taymiyah, 22/605).

Haatim (may Allah have mercy on him) said: "I carry out what I am commanded; I walk with fear of Allah in my heart; I start with the [correct] intention; I magnify and glorify Allah; I recite at a slow and measured pace, thinking about the meaning; I bow with khushoo'; I prostrate with humility; I sit and recite the complete tashahhud; I say salaam with the [correct] intention; I finish with sincerity towards Allah; and I come back fearing lest [my prayer] has not been accepted from me, so I continue to strive until I die." (Al-Khushoo' fi'l-Salaah, 27-28).

Abu Bakr al-Subghi said: "I lived through the time of two imaams (leaders) although I was not fortunate enough to hear them in person: Abu Haatim al-Raazi and Muhammad ibn Nasr al-Marwazi. As for Ibn Nasr, I do not know of any prayer better than his. I heard that a hornet stung him on his forehead and blood started flowing down his face, but he did not move." Muhammad ibn Ya'qoob al-Akhram said: "I have never seen any prayer better than that of Muhammad ibn Nasr. Flies used to land on his ears, and he did not shoo them away. We used to marvel at how good his prayer and khushoo' were. His fear [of Allah] in prayer was so great that he would put his chin on his chest as if he were a piece of wood standing up." (Ta'zeem Qadr al-Salaah, 1/58). Shaykh al-Islam Ibn Taymiyah (may Allah have mercy on him), when he started to pray, used to tremble so much that he would lean right and left. (Al-Kawaakib al-Durriyah fi Manaaqib al-Mujtahid Ibn Taymiyah, by Mar'i al-Karami, p. 83, Daar al-Gharb al-Islaami).

Compare this with what some of us do nowadays, looking at our watches, adjusting our clothes, fiddling with our noses, thinking of deals and counting our money whilst praying, or tracing the patterns of decorations on carpets and ceilings, or trying to see who is beside us. Think of how anyone would behave before some great leader of this world – would he dare to behave in such a manner then?!

Knowing the advantages of khushoo' in salaah

These include:

- The Prophet (peace and blessings of Allah be upon him) said: "There is no Muslim man who, when the time for a prescribed prayer comes, he does wudoo' properly, has the proper attitude of khushoo', and bows properly, but it will be an expiation for all his previous sins, so long as they were not major sins (kabeerah). And this is the case for life" (Reported by Muslim, 1/206, no. 7/4/2)

- The reward recorded is in proportion to the degree of khushoo', as the Prophet (peace and blessings of Allah be upon him) said: "A slave may pray and have nothing recorded for it except a tenth of it, or a ninth, or an eighth, or a seventh, or a sixth, or a fifth, or a quarter, or a third, or a half." (Reported by Imaam Ahmad; Saheeh al-Jaami', 1626).

- Only the parts of his prayer where he focused and concentrated properly will be of any avail to him. It was reported that Ibn 'Abbaas (may Allah be pleased with him) said: "You will only have from your prayer that which you focused on."

Sins will be forgiven if you concentrate properly and have full khushoo', as the Prophet (peace and blessings of Allah be upon him) said: "When a slave stands and prays, all his sins are brought and placed on his head and shoulders. Every time he bows or prostrates, some of them fall from him." (Reported by al-Bayhaqi in al-Sunan al-Kubraa, 3/10; see also Saheeh al-Jaami'). Al-Manaawi said: "What is meant is that every time a pillar (essential part) of the prayer is completed, part of his sins fall from him, until when he finishes his prayer, all his sins will be removed. This is in a prayer where all the conditions are met and the essential parts are complete. What we understand from the words "slave" and "stands" is that he is standing before the King of Kings [Allah] in the position of a humble slave." (Reported by al-Bayhaqi in al-Sunan al-Kubraa, 3/10; see also Saheeh al-Jaami').

- The one who prays with khushoo' will feel lighter when he finishes his prayer, as if his burdens have been lifted from him. He will feel at ease and refreshed, so that he will wish he had not stopped praying, because it is such a source of joy and comfort for him in this world. He will keep feeling that he is in a constricting prison until he starts to pray again; he will find comfort in prayer instead of wanting just to get it over and done with. Those who love prayer say: we pray and find comfort in our prayer, just as their leader, example and Prophet (peace and blessings of Allah be upon him) said, "O Bilaal, let us find comfort in prayer." He did not say "Let us get it over and done with."

- The Prophet (peace and blessings of Allah be upon him) said, "My joy has been made in prayer." So whoever finds his joy in prayer, how can he bear to look for joy anywhere else, or to keep away from it?

(Al-Waabil al-Sayib, 37).

Striving to offer du'a' at the appropriate times during the prayer, especially in sujood

There is no doubt that talking to Allah, humbling oneself before Him, asking things from Him and earnestly seeking His help, all help to strengthen the slave's ties to his Lord and increase his khushoo'. Du'aa' is an act of worship, and we are commanded to make du'a'. Allah says (interpretation of the meaning): "... call upon Him in humility and in secret..." [al-An'aam 6:63]. The Prophet (peace and blessings of Allah be upon him) said: "Whoever does not call on Allah, Allah will be angry with him." (Reported by al-Tirmidhi, Kitaab al-Da'waat, 1/426; classed as hasan in Saheeh al-Tirmidhi, 2686).

It was reported that the Prophet (peace and blessings of Allah be upon him) used to make du'a' at specific places in the prayer, i.e., in sujood, between the two prostrations and after the Tashahhud. The greatest of these is in sujood, because the Prophet (peace and blessings of Allah be upon him) said, "The closest that the slave can be to his Lord is when he is prostrating, so increase your du'a' [at that time]." (Reported by Muslim, Kitaab al-Salaah, Baab maa yuqaalu fi'l-rukoo' wa'l-sujood. No. 215). And he said: "... As for sujood, strive hard to make du'a' in it, for it is bound to be answered for you." (Reported by Muslim, Kitaab al-Salaah, Baab al-Nahy 'an qiraa'at al-Qur'an fi'l rukoo' wa'l-sujood, no. 207).

One of the du'aa's which the Prophet (peace and blessings of Allah be upon him) used to recite in his sujood was: "Allaahumma'ghfir li dhanbi diqqahu wa jillahu wa awwalahu wa aakhirahu wa 'alaaniyatahu wa sirrahu (O Allah, forgive me my sins, the minor and the major, the first and the last, the open and the hidden)." (Reported by Muslim, Kitaab al-Salaah, Baab ma yuqaalu fi'l-rukoo' wa'l-sujood, no. 216). He also used to say, "Allaahumma'ghfir li maa asrartu wa maa a'lantu (O Allah, forgive me what I have done in secret and done openly)." (Reported by al-Nisaa'i, al-Mujtabaa, 2/569; Saheeh al-Jaami', 1067).

We have already described some of the du'aa's that he used to recite between the two sajdahs. (See section 11).

One of the things that he (peace and blessings of Allah be upon him) used to recite after the Tashahhud is what we learn from the hadith: "When any one of you finishes the Tashahhud, let him seek refuge with Allah from four things, from the punishment of Hell, from the punishment of the grave, from the trials (fitnah) of life and death, and from the evil of the Dajjal ('Antichrist')." He used to say,

"Allaahumma innee a'oodhu bika min sharri maa 'amiltu wa min sharri maa lam a'mal (O Allah, I seek refuge with You from the evil of what I have done and the evil of what I have not done)."

"Allaahumma haasibni hisaaban yaseeran (O Allah, make my accounting easy)."

He taught Abu Bakr al-Siddeeq (may Allah be pleased with him) to say, "Allaahumma innee zalamtu nafsi zulman katheeran, wa la yaghfir al-dhunooba illa anta, faghfir li maghfiratan min 'indaka warhamni innaka anta al-Ghafoor al-Raheem (O Allah, I have wronged myself very much, and no one can forgive sin but You. Grant me forgiveness from You and have mercy on me, for You are the All-Forgiving, Most Merciful)."

He heard a man saying in his Tashahhud: "Allaahumma inne as'aluka yaa Allah al-Ahad al-Samad alladhi lam yalid wa lam yoolad wa lam yakum lahu kufuwan ahad an taghfir li dhunoobi innaka anta'l-Ghafoor al-Raheem (O Allah, I ask You O Allah, the One, the Self-Sufficient Master, Who begets not neither is begotten, and there is none like unto Him, to forgive me my sins, for You are the All-Forgiving, Most Merciful)." He (peace and blessings of Allah be upon him) said to his companions: "He has been forgiven, he has been forgiven."

He heard another man saying, "Allaahumma innee as'aluka bi-anna laka'l-hamd, laa ilaaha ill anta wahdaka laa shareeka lak al-Mannaan yaa badee' al-samawaati wa'l-ard, yaa dhaa'l-jalaali wa'l-ikraam, ya hayyu yaa qayyoom, innee as'aluka al-jannah wa a'oodhu bika min al-naar (O Allah, I ask You as all praise is due to You, there is no god but You Alone, with no partner or associate, the Bestower, O Originator of the heavens and earth, O Possessor of Glory and Honour, O Ever-Living, O Self-Sustaining, I ask You for Paradise and I seek refuge with You from Hell)." The Prophet (peace and blessings of Allah be upon him) said to his companions: "Do you know by what did he ask Allah?" They said, "Allah and His Messenger know best." He said, "By the One in Whose hand is my soul, he asked Allah by His greatest Name (ismuhu'l-a'zam) which, when He is called by it, He responds, and if He is asked by it, He gives."

The last thing he would say between the Tashahhud and the Tasleem was: "Allaahumma'aghfir li maa qaddamtu wa ma akhkhartu wa maa asrartu wa maa a'lantu wa maa asraftu wa maa anta a'lam bihi minni anta'l-muqaddim wa anta'l-mu'akhkhir, laa ilaaha illa anta (O Allah, forgive me what I have done in the past, and what I will do in the future, and what I have concealed, and what I have done openly, and what I have exceeded in, whatever You know about more than I. You are the Bringer-Forward, and You are the Delayer, there is no god except You)."

(These du'aa's and others, along with their isnaads, are to be found in Sifat al-Salaah by al-'Allaamah al-Albaani, p.163, 11th edn.)

Memorizing du'aa's like these will solve the problem that some people have of remaining silent behind the imaam when they have finished the Tashahhud because they do not know what they should say.

Adhkaar to be recited after prayer

These also help to strengthen khushoo' in the heart and reinforce the blessings and benefits of the prayer.

Without a doubt, one of the best ways of preserving and protecting a good action is to follow it up with another. So the one who thinks about the adhkaar that come after the prayer will find that they begin with seeking forgiveness three times, as if the worshipper is seeking forgiveness from his Lord for any shortcomings that may have occurred in his prayer or his khushoo'. It is also important to pay attention to naafil (supererogatory) prayers, because they make up for anything lacking in the fard (obligatory) prayers, including any failure with regard to khushoo'.

Having discussed things that help us to have khushoo', we now move on to a discussion of

Warding off distractions and things that adversely affect khushoo'

Removing anything that may distract the worshipper

Anas (may Allah be pleased with him) said: " 'Aa'ishah had a decorated, colourful curtain which she used to cover the side of her house. The Prophet (peace and blessings of Allah be upon him) said to her, 'Take it away from me, because its decorations keep distracting me when I pray.'" (Reported by al-Bukhari, Fath al-Baari, 10/391).

Al-Qaasim reported that 'Aa'ishah (may Allah be pleased with her) had a cloth with decorations on it, which she used to cover a small sunken alcove (used for sleeping or storage). The Prophet (peace and blessings of Allah be upon him) used to pray facing it, and he said, 'Take it away from me, because its decorations keep distracting me when I pray.' So she took it away and made pillows out of it." (Reported by Muslim in his Saheeh, 3/1668).

Another indication of this is the fact that when the Prophet (peace and blessings of Allah be upon him) entered the Ka'bah to pray in it, he saw two ram's horns. When he had prayed, he told 'Uthmaan al-Hajabi, "I forgot to tell you to cover the horns, because there should not be anything in the House to distract the worshipper." (Reported by Abu Dawood, 2030; Saheeh al-Jaami', 2504).

This also includes avoiding praying in places where people pass through, or where there is a lot of noise and voices of people talking, or where they are engaging in conversations, arguments etc., or where there are visual distractions.

One should also avoid praying in places that are very hot or very cold, if possible. The Prophet (peace and blessings of Allah be upon him) told us to delay praying Zuhr in summer until the hottest part of the day was over. Ibn al-Qayyim (may Allah have mercy on him) said: "Praying when it is intensely hot prevents a person from having the proper khushoo' and presence of mind, and he does his worship reluctantly, so the Prophet wisely told them to delay praying until the heat had lessened somewhat, so that they could pray with presence of mind and thus achieve the purpose of prayer, i.e., having khushoo' and turning to Allah." (Al-Waabil al-Sayib, Daar al-Bayaan edn., p.22)

Not praying in a garment that has decorations, writing, bright colours or pictures that will distract the worshipper

'Aa'ishah (may Allah be pleased with her) said: "The Prophet (peace and blessings of Allah be upon him) stood up to pray wearing a checkered shirt, and he looked at the patterns in it. When he had finished his prayer, he said, "Take this shirt to Abu Jaham ibn Hudhayfah and bring me an anbajaani (a garment with no decorations or checks), because it distracted me when I was praying." According to another report: "These checks distracted me." According to another report: "He had a checkered shirt, which used to distract him whilst he was praying." **(Reports in Saheeh Muslim, no. 556, part 3/391).**

It is better not to pray in a garment that has pictures on it, and we should be especially careful to avoid garments with pictures of animate beings, like many garments that are widely available nowadays.

Not praying when there is food prepared that one wants to eat

The Messenger of Allah (peace and blessings of Allah be upon him) said: "Do not pray when there is food prepared." **(Reported by Muslim, no. 560).**

If food has been prepared and served, or if it is offered, a person should eat first, because he will not be able to concentrate properly and have khushoo' if he leaves it and gets up to pray when he is wanting to eat. He should not even hasten to finish eating, because the Prophet (peace and blessings of Allah be upon him) said: "If the dinner is served and the time for prayer comes, eat dinner before praying Salaat al-Maghrib, and do not rush to finish your meal." **According to another report:** "If dinner has been put out and the iqaamah has been given for prayer, eat dinner first and do not rush to finish it." **(Agreed upon. Al-Bukhari, Kitaab al-Aadhan, Baab idhaa hadara al-ta'aamu wa uqeemat al-salaah; Muslim, no. 557-559).**

Not praying when one needs to answer the call of nature

No doubt one of the things that can prevent proper khushoo' is praying when one needs to go to the washroom. The Prophet (peace and blessings of Allah be upon him) forbade praying when one is suppressing the urge to urinate or defecate. **(Reported by Ibn Maajah in his Sunan, no. 617; Saheeh al-Jaami', no. 6832).**

If anyone is in this position, he should first go to the bathroom and answer the call of nature, even if he misses whatever he misses of the congregational prayer, because the Prophet (peace and blessings of Allah be upon him) said: "If any one of you needs to go to the toilet, and the prayer has begun, he should go to the toilet first." **(Reported by Abu Dawood, no. 88; Saheeh al-Jaami', no. 299)**

If this happens to a person whilst he is praying, he should stop praying, go and answer the call of nature, purify himself then pray, because the Prophet (peace and blessings of Allah be upon him) said, "There is no prayer when there is food prepared or if one is suppressing the urge to expel waste matter." **(Saheeh Muslim, no. 560).** Without a doubt, this trying to suppress the urge takes away khushoo'. This ruling also applies to suppressing the urge to pass wind.

Not praying when one feels sleepy

Anas ibn Maalik said, "The Messenger of Allah (peace and blessings of Allah be upon him) said: "If any one of you feels sleepy when he is praying, he should sleep until he [is rested enough to] know what he is saying," i.e., he should take a nap until he no longer feels drowsy. (Reported by al-Bukhari, no. 210).

This may happen when one is praying qiyaam al-layl, at the time when prayers are answered, and a person may pray against himself without realizing it. This hadith also includes fard prayers, when a person is confident that he will still have enough time to pray after taking a nap. (Fath al-Baari, Sharh Kitaab al-Wudoo', Baab al-wudoo' min al-nawm).

Not praying behind someone who is talking (or sleeping)

The Prophet (peace and blessings of Allah be upon him) forbade this; he said: "Do not pray behind one who is sleeping or one who is talking." (Reported by Abu Dawood, no. 694; Saheeh al-Jaami', no. 375. He said, a hasan hadith).

- because one who is talking will distract the worshipper with his talk, and one who is sleeping may expose something that will distract the worshipper.

Al-Khattaabi (may Allah have mercy on him) said: "As for praying behind people who are talking, al-Shaafa'i and Ahmad ibn Hanbal considered this to be makrooh, because their talk distracts the worshipper from his prayer." ('Awn al-Ma'bood, 2/388).

As regards not praying behind someone who is sleeping, a number of scholars thought that the evidence for this was weak (including Abu Dawood in his Sunan, Kitaab al-Salaah, Tafree' Abwaab al-Witr, Baab al-Du'aa', and Ibn Hajar in Fath al-Baari, Sharh Baab al-Salaah khalf al-Naa'im, Kitaab al-Salaah).

Al-Bukhari, may Allah have mercy on him, quoted the hadith of 'Aa'ishah in his Saheeh, Baab al-Salaah khalf al-Naa'im: "The Prophet (peace and blessings of Allah be upon him) used to pray whilst I was lying across from him on his bed..." (Saheeh al-Bukhari, Kitaab al-Salaah).

Mujaahid, Taawoos and Maalik thought it makrooh to pray facing someone who was sleeping, lest he expose something that would distract the worshipper from his prayer. (Fath al-Baari, ibid.)

If there is no risk of that happening, then it is not makrooh to pray behind someone who is sleeping. And Allah knows best.

Not occupying oneself with smoothing the ground in front of one

Al-Bukhari (may Allah have mercy on him) reported from Mu'ayqeeb (may Allah be pleased with him) that the Prophet (peace and blessings of Allah be upon him) said concerning a man's smoothing the ground when he prostrates, "If you have to do that, then do it only once." (Fath al-Baari, 3/79).

The Messenger of Allah (peace and blessings of Allah be upon him) said: "Do not wipe (the ground) when you are praying, but if you have to, then do it only once." (Reported by Abu Dawood, no. 946; Saheeh al-Jaami', no. 7452).

The reason for this prohibition is so as to maintain khushoo', and so that a person will not make too many extra movements in prayer. If the place where one is going to prostrate needs to be smoothed, it is better to do this before starting to pray.

This also applies to wiping the forehead or nose when praying. The Prophet (peace and blessings of Allah be upon him) used to prostrate in water and mud, which would leave traces on his forehead, but he did not bother to wipe it off every time he raised his head from sujood. It remained there because he was so deeply absorbed in his prayer and his khushoo' was so strong that he took not notice of it. The Prophet (peace and blessings of Allah be upon him) said: "Prayer is an occupation in itself." (Reported by al-Bukhari, Fath al-Baari, 3/72). Ibn Abi Shaybah reported that Abu'l-Darda' said: "Even if I were to get red camels, I would not like to wipe the gravel from my forehead." 'Ayaad said: "The salaf did not like to wipe their foreheads before they finished praying." (al-Fath, 3/79).

Just as a worshipper should avoid anything that will distract him from his prayer, by the same token he should avoid disturbing others. This includes:

Not disturbing others with one's recitation

The Messenger of Allah (peace and blessings of Allah be upon him) said: "All of you are speaking to your Lord, so do not disturb one another, and do not raise your voices above one another when reciting" or he said, "in prayer." (Reported by Abu Dawood, 2/83; Saheeh al-Jaami', no. 752). According to another report, he said, "Do not compete with one another in raising your voices when reciting Qur'an." (Reported by Imaam Ahmad, 2/36; Saheeh al-Jaami', 1951).

Not turning around during prayer

Abu Dharr (may Allah be pleased with him) said: "The Messenger of Allah (peace and blessings of Allah be upon him) said: 'Allah continues to turn towards His slave whilst he is praying, so long as he does not turn away, but if he turns away, [Allah] turns away from him." (Reported by Abu Dawood, no. 909; Saheeh Abi Dawood).

Turning away during prayer is of two types:

The turning away of the heart to something other than Allah.

The turning away of the eyes.

Both of them are not allowed, and are detrimental to the reward for the prayer. The Messenger of Allah (peace and blessings of Allah be upon him) was asked about turning away during prayer, and he said: "It is something that Shaytan steals from a person's prayer." (Reported by al-Bukhari, Kitaab al-Adhaan, Baab al-Iltifaat fi'l-Salaah).

The one who turns away with his heart or his eyes during prayer is like a man who is called by the ruler and made to stand before him, and when the ruler starts to address him, he turns away, looking to the right and the left, not listening to what the ruler is saying and not understanding a word of it, because his heart and mind are elsewhere. What does this man think the ruler will do to him?

The least that he deserves is that when he leaves the ruler, he is hated and no longer valued. One who prays like this is not equal to one who prays with the proper presence of mind, turning to Allah in his prayer in such a way that he feels the greatness of the One before Whom he is standing, and he is filled with fear and submission; he feels too shy before his Lord to turn to anyone else or to turn away. The difference between their prayers is as Hassaan ibn 'Atiyah said: "The two men may be in one congregation, but the difference in virtue between them is as great as the distance between heaven and earth. One of them is turning with all his heart towards Allah, whilst the other is negligent and forgetful." (Al-Waabil al-Sayib by Ibn al-Qayyim, Daar al-Bayaan, p. 36).

As for turning away for a genuine reason, this is OK. Abu Dawood reported that Sahl ibn al-Hanzaliyyah said: "We started praying – Salaat al-Subh (Fajr) – and the Messenger of Allah (peace and blessings of Allah be upon him) was looking at the ravine." Abu Dawood said: "He had sent a horseman at night to guard the ravine." This is like when he carried Umaamah bint Abi'l-'Aas, and when he opened the door for 'Aa'ishah, and when he came down from the minbar whilst praying in order to teach them, and when he stepped back during Salaat al-Kusoof (prayer at the time of an eclipse), and when he grabbed and strangled the Shaytan when he wanted to interrupt his prayer. He also ordered that snakes and scorpions should be killed even during prayer, and a person who is praying should stop and even fight one who wants to pass in front of him whilst he is praying. He told women to clap during prayer [if they spot a mistake on the part of the imaam], and he used to wave or gesture to people who greeted him whilst he was praying. These and other actions may be done in cases of necessity, but if there is no necessity, then they are just idle gestures that cancel out khushoo' and are therefore not allowed during prayer. (Majmoo' al-Fataawa, 22/559).

Not raising one's gaze to the heavens

The Prophet (peace and blessings of Allah be upon him) forbade us to do this and issued a warning against it. He said: "When any one of you is praying, he should not lift his gaze to the heavens, lest he lose his sight." (Reported by Ahmad, 5/294; Saheeh al-Jaami', no. 762). According to another report, he said: "What is wrong with people who lift their gaze to the heavens whilst they are praying?" According to another report, he said: "that they raise their gaze when they make du'a' during salaah?" (Reported by Muslim, no. 429). He spoke out strongly against it, to the extent that he said, "Let them stop it, or their eyesight will be taken away." (Reported by Imaam Ahmad, 5/258; Saheeh al-Jaami', 5574).

Not spitting in front of one when praying

This is incompatible with khushoo' and good manners before Allah. The Prophet (peace and blessings of Allah be upon him) said: "When any one of you is praying, let him not spit in front of himself, for Allah is before him when he prays." (Reported by al-Bukhari in his Saheeh, no. 397).

He also said: "When any one of you stands up to pray, he should not spit in front of himself, because he is talking to Allah – may He be blessed and exalted – as long as he is in his prayer place; and he should not [spit] to his right, because there is an angel on his right. He should spit to his left, or beneath his feet, and bury it." (Reported by al-Bukhari, al-Fath, no. 416, 1/512).

He said: "When one of you stands to pray, he is talking to his Lord, and his Lord is between him and the qiblah, so none of you should spit in the direction of his qiblah, but to his left or under his feet." (Reported by al-Bukhari, al-Fath al-Baari, no. 417, 1/513).

If the mosque is furnished with carpets and so on, as is the norm nowadays, if a person needs to spit, he can take out a handkerchief or whatever, spit into it, and put it away again.

Trying not to yawn when praying

The Messenger of Allah (peace and blessings of Allah be upon him) said: "If any one of you feels the urge to yawn during prayer, let him suppress it as much as he can, lest the Shaytan enter…" (Reported by Muslim, 4/2293). If the Shaytan enters, he will be more able to disturb the worshipper's khushoo', in addition to laughing at him when he yawns.

Not putting one's hands on one's hips when praying

Abu Hurayrah said: "The Messenger of Allah (peace and blessings of Allah be upon him) forbade putting the hands on the hips during prayer." (Reported by Abu Dawood, no. 947; Saheeh al-Bukhari, Kitaab al-'Aml fi'l-Salaah, Baab al-Hadhr fi'l-Salaah).

Ziyaad ibn Subayh al-Hanafi said: "I prayed beside Ibn 'Umar and I put my hand on my hip, but he struck my hand. When he had finished praying, he said, "This is crossing in prayer. The Messenger of Allah (peace and blessings of Allah be upon him) used to forbid this." (Reported by Imaam Ahmad, 2/106 and others. Classed as saheeh by al-Haafiz al-'Iraaqi in Takhreej al-Ihyaa'. See al-Irwaa', 2/94).

It was reported that the Prophet (peace and blessings of Allah be upon him) said that this posture is how the people of Hell rest; we seek refuge with Allah from that. (Reported by al-Bayhaqi from Abu Hurayrah. Al-'Iraaqi said, its isnaad appears to be saheeh).

Not letting one's clothes hang down (sadl) during prayer

It was reported that the Messenger of Allah (peace and blessings of Allah be upon him) forbade letting one's clothes hang down during prayer or for a man to cover his mouth. (Reported by Abu Dawood, no. 643; Saheeh al-Jaami', no. 6883. He said, this is a hasan hadith). In 'Awn al-Ma'bood (2/347) al-Khattaabi said: "Al-sadl: letting one's clothes hang down all the way to the ground." It was reported in Marqaat al-Mafaateeh (2/236): "Al-sadl is completely forbidden because it has to do with showing off, and in prayer it is even worse." The author of al-Nihaayah said: "It means wrapping oneself up in one's garment, leaving one's hands inside and bowing and prostrating in it." It was said that the Jews used to do this. It was also said that al-sadl meant putting the garment over one's head or shoulders, and letting its edges come down in front and over one's upper arms, so that a person will be preoccupied in taking care of it, which reduces khushoo', unlike garments that are tied up properly or buttoned, which do not distract the worshipper or affect his khushoo'. These kinds of clothes are still to be found nowadays in some parts of Africa and elsewhere, and in the way some Arabian cloaks are worn, which distract the worshipper and keep him busy adjusting them, retying them if they become loose and so on. This should be avoided.

The reason why it is forbidden to cover one's mouth was explained by the scholars as being because that prevents a person from reciting Qur'an and doing sujood properly. (Marqaat al-Mafaateeh, 2/236).

Not resembling animals

Allah has honoured the son of Adam and created him in the best way, so it is shameful for the son of Adam to resemble or imitate animals. We have been forbidden to resemble or imitate a number of postures or movements of animals when we pray, because that is contrary to khushoo' or because it is ugly and does not befit the worshipper who is praying. For example, it was reported that the Messenger of Allah (peace and blessings of Allah be upon him) forbade three things in prayer: pecking like a crow, spreading one's forearms like a carnivore, or always praying in the same place like a camel keeping to its own territory. (Reported by Ahmad, 3/428). It was said that when a man always prays in the same place in the mosque, making it his own, it is like a camel keeping to its own territory. (Al-Fath al-Rabaani, 4/91). According to another report: "He forbade me to peck like a cockerel, to sit like a dog or to turn like a fox." (Reported by Imaam Ahmad, 2/311; Saheeh al-Targheeb, no. 556).

This is what we were able to mention about the means of attaining khushoo', so that we may strive for them, and about the things that detract from khushoo', so that we can avoid them.

There is another issue that has to do with khushoo', to which the scholars attached so much importance that it is worthy of mention here:

When a person suffers a great deal of waswaas (insinuating thoughts from Shaytan) in his prayer, is his prayer valid or does he have to repeat it?

Ibn al-Qayyim, may Allah have mercy on him, said:

"It was said: what do you say concerning the prayer of one who has no khushoo', does he have to repeat it or not?

With regard to whether it will count for the purposes of reward, it will not be counted, except for [the parts] where one is focused and has the correct attitude of khushoo' towards one's Lord.

Ibn 'Abbaas said: 'You will gain nothing from your prayer except the parts where you were focused.'

In the Musnad it is reported that the Prophet (peace and blessings of Allah be upon him) said: "A person may offer a prayer, and nothing will be recorded of it for him except half of it, or a third, or a quarter ... or a tenth."

Allah has made the success of the worshipper in prayer dependent on his khushoo', and has indicated that the one who has no khushoo' will not be among the successful, but if it is counted for him for the purpose of reward, he will be one of the successful. With regard to the matter of whether it counts in terms of worldly rulings and exempts him from having to repeat it, if he focused with proper khushoo' for most of the prayer, it is OK, according to scholarly consensus. The sunnah prayers and adhkaar recited after prayer make up for anything that is lacking.

But in the case where there was no khushoo' or proper focus for most of the prayer, there is a difference of opinion among the fuqahaa'. Ibn Haamid, one of the companions of Ahmad, thought it obligatory to repeat the prayer. The fuqahaa' also differed with regard to khushoo' in prayer, and there are two scholarly opinions on this point. They are to be found in the Hanbali madhhab and others.

These opinions differ as to whether it is obligatory to repeat prayers in which one encountered a great deal of waswaas. Ibn Haamid among the companions of Ahmad said that it was obligatory, but the majority of fuqahaa' do not share this view.

They take as evidence the fact that the Prophet (peace and blessings of Allah be upon him) commanded the one who gets mixed up in his prayer to do sajdatay al-sahw (two prostrations of forgetfulness); he did not say that the prayer has to be repeated, even though he said, "The Shaytan comes to any one of you when he is praying and says, 'Remember such and such, remember such and such,' about something that he had forgotten, until he misguides him to the extent that he does not know how much he has prayed."

There is no dispute regarding the fact that there is no reward for the prayer except for the portion in which a person had proper presence of mind, as the Prophet (peace and blessings of Allah be upon him) said: "A person may offer a prayer, and nothing will be recorded of it for him except half of it, or a third, or a quarter … or a tenth."

Ibn 'Abbaas said: "You will gain nothing from your prayer except what you focus on." So [the prayer] is not correct if you are looking at it from the point of view that it has to be perfect, but it may be regarded as valid in the sense that we are not commanded to repeat it. (Madaarij al-Saalikeen, 1/112).

It was reported in al-Saheeh that the Prophet (peace and blessings of Allah be upon him) said: "When the muezzin calls the adhaan, the Shaytan runs away farting, so that he will not hear the adhaan. When the adhaan is over, he comes back. When the prayer starts, he runs away, but once it is in progress, he comes back, until he comes between a man and his own soul, and says, 'Remember such and such, remember such and such,' which he had forgotten, until he cannot remember how much he has prayed. If any one of you experiences this, let him do two prostrations of forgetfulness (sajdat al-sahw) whilst he is sitting."

They said: The Prophet (peace and blessings of Allah be upon him) commanded him, with regard to this prayer in which the Shaytan made him forget how much he had prayed, to do the two prostrations of forgetfulness. He did not command him to repeat it. If the prayer was invalid – as they claim – he would have told him to repeat it.

They said: This is the reason for the two prostrations of forgetfulness – to annoy the Shaytan for "whispering" insinuating thoughts to a person and coming between him and his own soul when he is praying. For this reason, these two prostrations are also called al-murghimatayn (the two annoying ones). (Madaarij al-Saalikeen, 1/528-530).

If you say that the prayer has to be repeated, so as to gain the benefits and rewards, then that is up to the individual. If he wants to gain those benefits, he can, and if he wants to miss out, he can.

If you say that we have to force people to repeat the prayer and punish them if they do not, applying to them the rulings on those who forsake prayer, then this is not right.

This is the more correct of the two opinions. And Allah knows best.

Conclusion

Khushoo' is a serious, major issue, which is impossible to achieve without the help of Allah. Being deprived of khushoo' is nothing short of a calamity. Hence the Prophet (peace and blessings of Allah be upon him) used to say in his du'a': "*Allaahumma innee a'oodhu bika min qalbin laa yakhsha'...* (O Allah, I seek refuge with You from a heart that has no khushoo'...)." (Reported by al-Tirmidhi, 5/485, no. 3482; Saheeh Sunan al-Tirmidhi, 2769).

Those who have khushoo' are of varying levels or degrees. Khushoo' is an action of the heart that may increase and decrease. Some people have khushoo' as great as the clouds of the sky, and others may finish their prayer without having understood anything at all.

"When it comes to prayer, people are of five levels:

The first is the level of the one who wrongs himself and is negligent. He does not do wudoo' properly, or pray at the right time or make sure he does all the necessary parts of prayer.

The second is one who observes the outward essentials of prayer, prays on time and does wudoo', but he has lost the battle against his own self and is overwhelmed with waswaas.

The third is one who observes the outward essentials of prayer, prays on time and does wudoo', and also strives against his own self and against waswaas, but he is preoccupied with his struggle against his enemy (i.e. the Shaytan), lest he steal from his prayer, so he is engaged in salaah and jihad at the same time.

The fourth is one who when he stands up to pray, he fulfils all the requirements of the prayer, and his heart is fully focused and alert lest he omit anything, and his concern is to do the prayer properly and perfectly. His heart is deeply immersed in his prayer and worship of his Lord.

The fifth is one who does all of that, but he takes his heart and places it before his Lord, looking at his Lord with his heart and focusing on Him, filled with love and adoration, as if he is actually seeing Him. That waswaas and those thoughts diminish, and the barriers between him and his Lord are lifted. The difference between the prayer of this person and the prayer of anyone is else is greater than the difference between heaven and earth. When this person prays, he is preoccupied with his Lord and content with Him.

The first type is punishable; the second is accountable; the third is striving so he is not counted as a sinner; the fourth is rewarded and the fifth is drawn close to his Lord, because he is one of those for whom prayer is a source of joy. Whoever finds their joy in prayer in this life, will find their joy in being close to Allah in the Hereafter, and will also find his joy in Allah in this world. Whoever finds his joy in Allah will be content with everything, and whoever does not find his joy in Allah, will be destroyed by his feelings of grief and regret for worldly matters."

(al-Waabil al-Sayib, p. 40).

Finally, we ask Allah to make us among those who have khushoo' and to accept our repentance. May He reward with good all those who helped to prepare this book and may He benefit all those who read it; Aameen. All praise be to Allah, Lord of the Worlds.

www.ingramcontent.com/pod-product-compliance
Lightning Source LLC
LaVergne TN
LVHW020447080526
838202LV00055B/5363